Coded Messages

Evangelism and The Da Vinci Code

Steve Hollinghurst

Researcher in Evangelism to Post-Christian Culture,
Church Army, Sheffield Centre

GROVE BOOKS LIMITED
RIDLEY HALL RD CAMBRIDGE CB3 9HU

Contents

Church Army supports the Grove Evangelism Series

Church Army is a society of evangelists within the Anglican Communion that trains, supports and deploys evangelists across the UK and Ireland to enable people to come to a living faith in Jesus Christ.

Church Army—sharing faith through words and action

For more information about church Army go to www.churcharmy.org.uk or phone 0208 309 3519 or email info@churcharmy.org.uk

Church Army, Marlowe House, 109 Station Rd, Sidcup, Kent DA15 7AD
Registered Charity number: 226226

The Cover Illustration is by Peter Ashton

First Impression February 2006
ISSN 1367-0840
ISBN 1 85174 614 5

Introduction

1

So Why Write Yet Another Response to this Book?

A lot has already been written about Dan Brown's best seller *The Da Vinci Code*. Most of this has been centred on the accuracy of information within the book. This is not the major subject of this booklet, though at the end I briefly list key 'facts' and suggest sources for further information.

In a programme exploring *The Da Vinci Code* broadcast on the 29th of September by ITV[1] it was amply shown that those attracted to the theories put forward by the characters in Brown's novel remain unconvinced by the welter of experts who have challenged their factual basis. The following quotes from the BBC website are typical of the reaction of many to the debate surrounding the book.

> On a recent plane journey, my husband and I scanned the books that passengers were reading. A clear third of them were nose deep into a Dan Brown book. Clearly his 'historical' claims have grabbed the attention of today's society. No more do people sit down and just take things as the truth when it comes to religious and political issues. Whether the 'facts' in *The Da Vinci Code* are indeed factual or if they truly belong on the fiction list, one thing is certain—it has made a lot of us sit up, pay attention and question what has been handed down to us from the church for hundreds of years. Hoorah to Dan Brown for that.
>
> Canada

> The claims in *The Da Vinci Code* are just as plausible as the claims in the Bible. No modern Christian has actually seen God, or Jesus, in the flesh, and yet they can claim their beliefs as truth. Why should the same not apply to the book? The trouble is, religious zealots are too closed minded to accurately question their own views.
>
> Stafford, UK

> It took almost a thousand years after Jesus passed away for the Grail story to appear. What was happening to the knowledge of the Grail during that time and why was such an important section of the life of Christ never referred to beforehand? Either the original Grail story is a

well-crafted fabrication or the Christian church is covering something up. The more the church protests, the more I feel they are concerned the truth will be revealed.

Stoke on Trent, Britain

I enjoyed reading the novel as a work of fiction based around some historical fact and ideas. However, the debate that I think is more worthwhile discussing rather than Da Vinci's role in the Holy Grail is the concept of Jesus' relationship with Mary Magdalene. He may be considered the Son of God, but he was still a man.

London, UK

The facts speak for themselves, as the saying goes, there's no smoke without fire.

Dudley, West Midlands, UK

In the last three years Dan Brown's novel has sold over 40 million copies world wide and is still a big seller. For some, Catholic journalist Sandra Meisel's conclusion about the book rings true:

Brown's Mess

In the end, Dan Brown has penned a poorly written, atrociously researched mess. So, why bother with such a close reading of a worthless novel? The answer is simple: *The Da Vinci Code* takes esoterica mainstream. It may well do for Gnosticism what *The Mists of Avalon* did for paganism—gain it popular acceptance. After all, how many lay readers will see the blazing inaccuracies put forward as buried truths?

What's more, in making phoney claims of scholarship, Brown's book infects readers with a virulent hostility toward Catholicism. Dozens of occult history books, conveniently cross-linked by Amazon.com, are following in its wake. And booksellers' shelves now bulge with falsehoods few would be buying without *The Da Vinci Code* connection. While Brown's assault on the Catholic Church may be a backhanded compliment, it's one we would have happily done without.[2]

However, for many others, *The Da Vinci Code*'s appeal does not in the end rest on its accuracy but in the attraction of the worldview it presents, a worldview that seems to many far more believable than their understanding of the Christian faith and certainly one that fits better with their experience and lifestyle.

Dan Brown himself makes several interesting comments about the controversy on his website:

The ideas in this novel have been around for centuries; they are not my own. Admittedly, this may be the first time these ideas have been written about within the context of a popular thriller, but the information is anything but new. My hope for *The Da Vinci Code* was, in addition to entertaining people, that it might serve as an open door for readers to begin their own explorations and rekindle their interest in topics of faith.

Many people in organized religion have come out in support of this novel, and, of course, many have come out in opposition as well. The opposition generally comes from the strictest Christian thinkers who feel the idea of a 'married Jesus' serves to undermine his divinity. While I don't agree with this interpretation, this is immaterial because the dialogue itself is a deeply empowering and positive force for everyone involved. Suddenly, enormous numbers of people are passionately debating important philosophical topics, and regardless of the personal conclusions that each of us draws, the debate can only help to strengthen our understanding of our own faith.

For me, whilst the debate about the facts is relevant, the real challenge for Christians is to enter into this debate, to engage in mission within the worldview of the book and effectively communicate the Christian faith within what we might call 'code culture.' This booklet is intended to help people understand this culture, why the debate about the facts is having little impact and at times may be counterproductive, and get to grips with the appeal of the book's key messages. It hopefully will also help Christians to communicate the Christian faith effectively within a society in which, as Dan Brown hoped, this book is stimulating a lot of religious debate. Finally, it offers suggestions for running events that can draw on the book's success as an opportunity to explore the Christian faith.

The real challenge for Christians is to enter into this debate, to engage in mission within what we might call 'code culture'

2

'Code Culture' and Society

In ITV's 'The Grail Trail; in pursuit of the Da Vinci Code,'
three fans of the book, Leah a 30-year-old lapsed Catholic,
Neil a 48-year-old and also a lapsed Catholic, and Philip,
a 24-year-old American training for ministry at Wycliffe
Hall, Oxford, are sent to visit the places in the book and meet
experts on the way.

Their progress is observed by Dr Raj Persaud, a psychologist, who analyses their behaviour. Both Leah and Neil share the negative opinions of the Catholic church put over in Brown's novel, preferring its alternative view of early Christianity. Philip is seeking evidence to support more traditional Christian belief. The experts range from a priest from Opus Dei, through several academic experts of no declared affiliation to a professor of history who is a practising Pagan and a writer who has been a source for some of the novel's ideas. The mix sheds some light on the 'facts' but turns out to shed even more illumination on why the book has proved so attractive in contemporary society.

Near the programme's conclusion Raj Persaud notes that

> 50 to 100 years ago we were bound together by a common religion...now all that binds us together is popular culture. *The Da Vinci Code*, because it has sold millions, is part of that culture and is the only thing that binds these people together even though they are all otherwise interested in religion.

Earlier he says of the three, 'these people are in many ways typical of millions today who are looking for new religious ideas, and the presence of these in the book is one of its greatest attractions.'

I think Dr Persaud is right. It is not that everyone today is inclined to believe the novel's claims or find its ideas attractive. However, a large number are and I think that has a lot to do with our culture in the early 21st century. What are the cultural elements that provide fertile soil for the book to be received within?

Rising Openness to Alternative Spirituality

David Hay has charted the changing fortunes of belief in the spiritual amongst those who do not go to church through surveys. In 1987 48% of respondents said they had had a spiritual or religious experience. This had risen to 76% in 2000.[3] Yet the understanding of such experiences had shifted away from traditional approaches to more alternative ones.

In 1987 27% reported feeling the presence of God, and almost the same number (29%) reported a sense that the events of their life where patterned by supernatural or spiritual forces. In 2000 those reporting an awareness of God's presence had risen to 38% but had been far outstripped by a sense that events were patterned by supernatural or spiritual forces which had risen to 55% of all respondents. Similarly the 'Soul of Britain' survey done for the BBC by ORB in 2000 showed that whilst 70% of people claimed to believe in God almost twice as many of these saw God as a spirit or life force, something akin to the 'Force' in Star Wars, than as a personal deity with whom one could have a relationship.

Sales in books under the Mind, Body, Spirit and Occult categories now outsell books on all of the traditional religions combined. Similarly belief in re-incarnation is equally as popular as belief in some form of heaven. As I have argued elsewhere in more depth, the apparent shift in culture from a modernist one (in which religion is marginalized and ultimately threatened with extinction by rationalist science) to a postmodern one (in which all ideas become subjective) has allowed the 'religious' to regain ground in mainstream culture.[4] But, if this is the case, it seems that this advantages new forms of spirituality over traditional religions.

Sales in books under the Mind, Body, Spirit and Occult categories now outsell books on all of the traditional religions combined

Suspicion of Experts and Authority Figures

In ITV's 'The Grail Trail' one of the notable things is the way the three 'pilgrims' often reject the opinions of the experts in favour of their own prior belief or instinct. Raj Persaud notes that 'people today have been taught to trust their own feelings over the views of authority figures.'

A notable example is when they discuss Leonardo Da Vinci's 'Last Supper' in Milan with an expert on his paintings. All three are convinced that it clearly depicts a woman at Jesus right hand. Like Brown they are also struck by the supposed V and M shapes made by the positioning of Jesus and 'Mary.' The expert does not agree. He is prepared to suggest that John may have been pictured as very effeminate partly due to Leonardo's homosexuality, but assures them it is not Mary and that there is no hidden symbolism in the shape, merely a compositional device. The three reject his view preferring their own reading of the picture.

Neil's underlying worldview tells him there is no such thing as 'an independent expert'

The conversation becomes particularly revealing when Neil asks the expert about his beliefs. The expert refuses to reveal them, insisting they are irrelevant to his view on Leonardo as an independent expert. Neil will not accept this saying, 'so I'll take it from that you are a committed Catholic then.' Neil's underlying worldview tells him there is no such thing as 'an independent expert'; rather, experts are seen as using their knowledge to represent subjective opinions. The expert's statement that his beliefs are not relevant so he will not share them is taken as the opposite of the truth; he is viewed instead as deliberately trying to cover up his bias.

The mistrust of authority figures and experts is not unique to this debate. What do we think when a scientist comes on TV to tell us it is perfectly safe to 'X' or there is no danger from a particular drug or treatment? Many will assume the opposite must be true and want to know who is paying the scientist. How many would now assume a politician is really serving our best interest rather than party spin and political expediency? Our scepticism is proved right often enough to justify it.

Nietzsche, the grandfather of postmodern thought, viewed all human behaviour as ruled by 'the Will to Power.' Even supposedly altruistic acts were really motivated by the self-interest of those performing them, whether they admitted it to themselves or not. From such a viewpoint an attempt by someone to convince you of their opinion or to accept a particular truth is in reality an attempt by them to dominate you and make you serve their ends. Even if we do live in a postmodern world only some would go as far as Nietzsche. However, many seem at least in part to share his view, particularly when it comes to how we see authority figures and experts, or anyone with strongly held beliefs. This inclination re-enforces the rejection of traditional religion, which is often viewed as authoritarian and rigid, in favour of beliefs linked to personal spirituality and centred on one's own experience. Religious leaders or theological experts are likely to be viewed as suspect.

Belief in Conspiracy Theories

In the discussion over Da Vinci's 'Last Supper' mentioned above Neil moved quickly from a mistrust of the expert to a belief he was deliberately trying to hide things to further his own ends. If our culture mistrusts the experts and authority figures it also is inclined to believe in cover-ups and conspiracies.

You can find people seriously believing any of the following conspiracy theories. The US Air force has been making regular contact with aliens since WW2, and the evidence is hidden in 'the blue room' in a secret location in Area 51. Often linked to this is the supposed 'Roswell incident' in which an alien craft crashed and the aliens' bodies then examined. The US government is deliberately hiding this and using tests of new aircraft as a smokescreen. Staying in this area are reported sightings of 'Men in Black' who mysteriously turn up at key events or abduct people onto spacecraft. Others have argued in detail that the moon landings never happened; they were faked on earth as a part of a cold war propaganda exercise to trump the Russians who were in reality ahead in the space race. For years people have discussed the Bilderberg group, a meeting of high powered executives and leaders, who are accused of pulling the strings of all major world governments and organizations. They are variously linked to a whole raft of occult or secret groups or political ideologies. There are similar theories about the New World Order.

Other theories have apparently more ancient roots. The Knights Templar often feature, and there are numerous takes on the supposed secret power or treasure they are alleged to have discovered under King Solomon's temple. This is then variously linked to their suppression on the grounds of devil worship. Other groups who regularly emerge are the Rosicrucians and the Freemasons. Often various artists and thinkers, occult, political or scientific figures like Cornelius Agrippa, John Dee, Shakespeare, Leonardo Da Vinci, Isaac Newton and indeed all of the US founding fathers are connected with international cults secretly running the world or alternatively guarding powerful secrets that are the key to resisting the powers of evil seeking world domination. For some these are the source of entertaining plots in books and TV shows; for others they are living reality. The classic tale would be that of Timothy McVeigh who blew up the government building in Oklahoma City believing it to be a centre for the New World Order.[5]

It is easy for those who do not watch the shows or read the books to dismiss all of this as unbelievable nonsense, but actually much of it is argued very convincingly with recourse to numerous facts. And whilst some of the facts do not stand up well to scrutiny often many do. The issue is about how they are connected.

A mindset once limited to a minority has become far more mainstream. The worldview it inhabits tends to deny accident and chance and prefers instead to view everything as

A mindset once limited to a minority has become far more mainstream

having a meaning or purpose. Events that happen in the same place are thus probably linked. Things that look similar must also be linked. Add to this an assumption that the experts have something to hide, and denials of these links are viewed as confirmations of a conspiracy to cover them. This in turn must indicate that those who have spotted these links must be on to something. This is why people, like those quoted earlier in my introduction, find *The Da Vinci Code* so convincing.

As a teenager I used to read many books like this and believed a good proportion of them. As someone with a critical mind I also noted that not all of these agreed and I was able to compare different theories and come to my own conclusions, which added to my conviction that there was something in all this. In hindsight I have become aware how the occult mindset I had adopted had led to the continuous tendency to assume things must be connected and to see all sorts of things as 'proof.' I would add that Christians live in the same culture and are not necessarily immune to such conspiracy/occult thought.

The world of conspiracy in *The Da Vinci Code* is best exposed by another novel on the same area, *Foucault's Pendulum* by Umberto Eco.[6] The book is set in an Italian publishing house that specializes in the kind of occult and spirituality books we are talking about. The bored and sceptical editors believe none of it, but when they get a supposed secret document from a mysterious colonel they decide to have some fun and make some money. They feed random bits of 'secret information' and other theories and facts into a computer that can generate connections between almost anything. Readers of *The Da Vinci Code* would recognize much of the material. Using this they begin publishing books pointing to a compelling conspiracy and hidden occult secrets of power. Unfortunately their game is taken as truth by their readers who begin to pursue the secrets in order to unlock their power. People are killed and the editors are pursued. Attempts to expose the true source of the books simply convince others even more that the editors are hiding occult secrets. The publisher's joke is fast becoming a dangerous reality. What, I wonder, would happen if Dan Brown were to admit *The Da Vinci Code* was a joke? Would convinced readers simply drop the book's theories? Or might they wonder what Brown was trying to hide or which organization was forcing him to say this?

The Da Vinci Code and Contemporary Culture

Brown's book pushes all the right cultural buttons.

- It offers an alternative religious history and supports new spiritualities.
- It attacks a church that is viewed as authoritarian, dogmatic and sexist.

- It exposes a conspiracy by that church to suppress the truth and repress all forms of independent spiritual searching, especially belief in the sacred feminine and the place of women in religion.
- It ties all sorts of information, mysterious groups and historical incidents together in support of the book's ideas.
- It wraps this entire mix up with action, suspense and romance.

All of this is not only likely to make the book popular, but will convince many today that much of it is likely to be based on truth.

Further to this, 'code culture' means that, however many experts dismiss the truth of the book's claims, many will react like Leah in the ITV programme who at its close concludes, 'It's all a matter of opinion in the end. Having met lots of knowledgeable people it all comes down to their thoughts and their beliefs, and I don't really care in the end…I still think about 40% to 50% is true.' More difficult still for Christians seeking to respond to Brown's book is that 'code culture' also means that they are expected to try and attack the book as part of the church's conspiracy to suppress the truth it uncovers. The more Christians seek to prove the book wrong, especially if they do so with passion or sarcasm or aggression, or protest against it, denounce it, or try to ban it, the more they convince people that the book must be right.

The more Christians seek to prove the book wrong, the more they convince people that the book must be right

3 The Message of The Da Vinci Code

If you looked at the way some Christians have responded to the book, you would be forgiven for thinking that its sole purpose was to attack the Christian faith and the Roman Catholic Church in particular.

It may surprise people to learn that Brown sees himself as a Christian and that many of his key influences are also Christian theologians, both Catholic and Protestant. That 'being a Christian' means different things to different people, however, is something he acknowledges. The following are taken from his website.[7]

Are You a Christian?

Yes. Interestingly, if you ask three people what it means to be Christian, you will get three different answers. Some feel being baptized is sufficient. Others feel you must accept the Bible as absolute historical fact. Still others require a belief that all those who do not accept Christ as their personal saviour are doomed to hell. Faith is a continuum, and we each fall on that line where we may. By attempting to rigidly classify ethereal concepts like faith, we end up debating semantics to the point where we entirely miss the obvious—that is, that we are all trying to decipher life's big mysteries, and we are each following our own paths of enlightenment. I consider myself a student of many religions. The more I learn, the more questions I have. For me, the spiritual quest will be a life-long work in progress.

Is This Book Anti-Christian?

No. This book is not anti-anything. It's a novel. I wrote this story in an effort to explore certain aspects of Christian history that interest me. The vast majority of devout Christians understand this fact and consider *The Da Vinci Code* an entertaining story that promotes spiritual discussion and debate. Even so, a small but vocal group of individuals has proclaimed the story dangerous, heretical, and anti-Christian. While I regret having offended those individuals, I should mention that priests, nuns, and clergy contact me all the time to thank me for writing the novel. Many church officials are celebrating *The Da Vinci Code* because it has sparked renewed interest in important topics of faith and Christian history. It is important to remember that a reader does not have to agree with every word in the novel to use the book as a positive catalyst for introspection and exploration of our faith.

In many ways it is probably more accurate to view Brown as seeking to change Christianity rather than seek its demise. True, both in this book and his preceding novels, he promotes a Christianity that tends to be inclusive of traditionally non-Christian spiritualities and embraces readings of Christian history that favour groups often considered heretical, but he is positive about Christian characters who are progressive and inclusive.[8] Both the murdered scientist who is also a devout Christian and the cardinal who eventually becomes Pope, are viewed very positively in *Angels and Demons*, the first Robert Langdon novel.

I suspect Brown sees himself as promoting a version of the Christian faith more likely to appeal within today's culture. Whether one considers Brown's revised Christian history accurate, or its revised beliefs consistent with the Christian faith, that it is far more appealing to many than what is seen as 'traditional Christianity' is difficult to dispute. This is why I think, in responding to the book evangelistically, we need to take Brown's revised Christianity seriously, even if we do not agree with it. Brown has clearly put his finger on issues that are of importance to the way the Christian faith comes across in contemporary culture.

Brown's Alternative Christianity

If Brown pushes one big theme in his books I think it is restoring 'the sacred feminine' to religion and in particular to a Christianity he believes once embraced it. But note this comment on his website:

Two thousand years ago, we lived in a world of Gods and Goddesses. Today, we live in a world solely of Gods. Women in most cultures have been stripped of their spiritual power. The novel touches on questions of how and why this shift occurred…and on what lessons we might learn from it regarding our future.

The sacred feminine is not only a plot feature for the book—Brown devotes pages to long discussions about it. The hero, Robert Langdon, is going to meet the head of the Louvre, Jacques Saunière; on the evening the latter is killed because both are passionate scholars of goddess tradition.[9] When the police chief Fache is showing Sauniere's body to Langdon, the pentacle drawn upon it becomes the start of a two page description of its origins as a pre-Christian Pagan representation of the divine feminine in nature, its links to the trajectory of the planet Venus, and the Olympics. When Fache suggests it is a symbol of devil worship, Langdon explains how it is not, but the church deliberately took positive Pagan symbols and made them satanic in order to attack Pagans.[10]

Later discovery of clues to Leonardo Da Vinci prompt a discussion in which Langdon links the artist and the murdered Sauniere together as believers in nature religion passionately opposed to the church's suppression of the divine feminine.[11] Further he suggests that Leonardo's paintings, even those of ostensibly Christian subjects, are in fact full of clues promoting goddess religion.

Most of chapter 20 is devoted to Langdon telling the heroine, Sauniere's grand-daughter Sophie, about how the Tarot is in fact a text promoting the sacred feminine, how all of life is structured around a divine proportion which is also a representation of the sacred feminine and lists a string of artists, musicians and thinkers inspired by this.[12] In part of this he recalls a lecture he delivered at Harvard in which he declares

My friends, as you can see, the chaos of the world has an underlying order. When the ancients discovered PHI, they were certain they had stumbled across God's building block for the world, and they worshipped nature because of that.[13] And one can understand why. God's hand is evident in Nature, and even to this day there exist pagan, Mother Earth-revering religions. Many of us celebrate Nature the way the pagans did, and don't even know it. May Day is a perfect example, the celebration of spring…the earth coming back to life to produce her bounty. The mysterious magic inherent in the Divine Proportion was written at the beginning of time.[14]

The Priory of Sion, of which Sauniere was head, is described by Langdon as the Pagan goddess worship cult, promoting feminine deities and having contempt for the church. We also hear that this group has been headed by 'some of history's most cultured individuals: men like Botticelli, Sir Isaac Newton and Victor Hugo' and, of course, Leonardo Da Vinci.[15] Throughout the book Langdon, and then the historian Teabing, promotes goddess worship and the sacred feminine.

In contrast to the positive advocacy of the Priory and Pagan beliefs and goddess worship, the church is portrayed as the opponent of this true faith. So Langdon explains to Sophie:

The priory's tradition of perpetuating goddess worship is based on a belief that powerful men in the early Christian church 'conned' the world by propagating lies that devalued the female and tipped the scales in favour of the masculine…The priory believes that Constantine and his male successors successfully converted the world from matriarchal paganism to patriarchal Christianity by waging a campaign of propaganda that demonized the sacred feminine, obliterating the goddess from modern religion forever.[16]

Langdon then begins two pages of private thought which he begins 'Nobody could deny the enormous good the modern church did in today's troubled world,' and yet the church had a violent and deceitful history'; the rest of those pages are devoted to recounting that history. This begins with the inquisition as a three-century long attack on women in which he claims 5 million were burned as witches.[17]

The doctrine of original sin is seen as an attack on the sacred feminine. He sees the church as having successfully driven women out of religion and as reclassifying sex, once an essential part of communing with God, as sinful and shameful.[18] Women have been cast as accomplices of the devil and their 'left brain' thinking cast as 'sinister' as opposed to *right*eousness which was male and right-brained. His thoughts finish by lamenting the demise of the goddess and viewing the Christian millennia as dominated by war, destruction, misogyny and environmental disaster as a result.

The idea of the church attacking sex is discussed further when Langdon explains a sex ritual called Heiros Gamos to Sophie.[19] He argues that in ancient religion women were sacred because they gave birth to life and men could only become spiritually complete by having sex, the point of climax being a moment of total communion with God. He goes on to claim that ritual prostitution was practised in the Jerusalem temple for this reason. The church and other religions he claims have thus always demonized sex because it broke their monopoly on access to God, enabling any ordinary person to commune with the divine, and thus sex undermined the church's power. He concludes with another reminiscence of his lectures at Harvard which ends with him advising the male students 'the next time you find yourself with a woman, look into your heart and see if you cannot approach sex as a mystical act. Challenge yourself to find that spark of divinity that a man can only achieve through union with the sacred feminine.'[20]

As part of the ITV programme the three pilgrims are taken by Ancient History professor and Pagan, Ronald Hutton, to see a symbolic enactment of Heiros Gamos by a group of Wiccans. Clearly Neil, who has already declared that reading *The Da Vinci Code* has made him want to explore becoming a Pagan, finds the experience inspiring. His fellow lapsed Catholic Leah on the other hand finds the whole thing laughable, and cannot see how sex can be an act of communion with God. Interestingly, she is an avid reader of New Age books and has come at the Code from this angle and is not attracted to Paganism in the way Neil is.[21] With the book's advocacy of goddess worship and Paganism I found it no surprise that someone might want to explore Paganism after reading it. This led me to wonder how contemporary Pagans viewed the book. I was helped in this by a web discussion set up amongst a British Pagan group on my behalf. The respondents were not sure that they welcomed all of Brown's treatment of the subject, some seeing it as raising a helpful discussion of the area but others as demeaning the real thing.

However, if Brown's agenda is a revised Christianity, in Britain at least he may actually end up attracting people to New Age and Paganism, even if the Pagans are not over keen on the ideas some new members might bring!

Ambiguity about the Church

If the church of the past is accused of death, lies and oppression, Brown seems more ambiguous about the church today. Usually in discussions Langdon and Teabing agree in the book. However, when Teabing suggests the church must be responsible for the murder of Sauniere and the other two heads of the Priory, Langdon clearly doubts this, remembering positively the new Pope and cardinals he met in the previous novel, *Angels and Demons*.[22] The problem for the reader at this point is that Teabing will be seen as telling the truth; a monk from Opus Dei has indeed murdered the three and is seeking the Priory's secret in order to destroy it as Teabing claims.

However, Langdon's doubts are, I think, closer to Brown's opinion. He is using Opus Dei as a group wedded to the church's traditions and thus still serving its violent and anti-goddess past as opposed to other Christians who are opening up to more modern inclusive ideas. Indeed, after the plot has reached its final revelations, the actions of the monk Silas are also not blamed fully on Opus Dei . The organisation's leader in the novel, Bishop Aringarosa, comes out as having wrong beliefs but not as condoning murder in support of those beliefs. In other places Langdon and Teabing claim that Christian scholars all know the truth, but the masses still ignorantly believe the traditional understanding of Jesus.

The depiction of Opus Dei is a plot device to warn the reader that the spirit of those who attacked the sacred feminine is alive and well in the church of today. So Sister Sandrine, a Catholic nun who in the book looks after St Sulpice in Paris and is also a member of the Priory, reflects on how Opus Dei not only still believes in bodily mortification but expects women to have to practice this more than men due to original sin. She also recites a list of inequalities in the way male and female members of Opus Dei are treated.[23]

At various points we get graphic descriptions of Silas practising bodily mortification until he bleeds, something Brown's positive characters clearly cannot equate with a good God.[24] Bishop Aringarosa is depicted as an opponent of the new Pope (whom Brown has depicted positively), modernization, Vatican II and any attempt by the church to accommodate the agendas of contemporary society. He also believes science and faith to be incompatible, advocating faith as not needing proof and unbiased science as impossible for anyone of faith to undertake.[25] The bishop blames liberalization for the decline of the church and claims people need firm direction and clear instruction from the church not indulgence of their agendas.[26]

Revising History

It is against this backdrop that Brown offers his central device to revise Christian history and reintroduce the sacred feminine—the true meaning of the Holy Grail.

For this he draws heavily on the Priory of Sion documents in the Paris national library and the interpretation of them found in *The Holy Blood and the Holy Grail*.[27] These claim that the true Grail was not the chalice from the Last Supper, but the blood of Christ as carried on through direct descendents of Jesus from his marriage to Mary Magdalene. This bloodline was intended to restore a Davidic king to Israel but this was not possible after Jesus' death so Mary fled to France with their daughter, Sarah. However, the Merovingian kings of France were her descendents, and the Priory of Sion holds documents proving Jesus' marriage, and to this day hides the identity of the true descendents of Christ.

Brown's characters offer other evidence for this. Already mentioned is the interpretation that Leonardo Da Vinci's paintings tell of this. So Mary is at Jesus' right in the Last Supper, not John; she and Jesus form a V shape, symbolizing a chalice, and an M shape pointing to Mary as the true Chalice, bearing Jesus' blood. Peter, it is claimed, is depicted threatening Mary as the two are rivals to run the church. The Gnostic gospels and Dead Sea Scrolls are cited as ancient texts that show that the early church also believed Mary had married Jesus and that she was the true leader of the early church. It was this Langdon and Teabing claim that the church after Constantine sought to suppress, re-writing Scripture to give us the four false gospels, in order to place Peter as the leader of the church and drive out the sacred feminine. Similarly, we are told how the Pope later recasts Mary as a prostitute to smear her character.[28]

Brown is not alone in proposing such a revision of church history, he has drawn heavily here on Catholic theologian Margaret Starbird. Her support for Brown is clear on her website[29] and Dan Brown's bibliography for the Code[30] lists several of Starbird's books. The write up on her site for one, *Magdalene's Lost Legacy*, reads like a plot using the kind of coded messages in Brown's book:

> Here Starbird explodes the myth of the celibate Jesus, revealing truths encoded in symbolic numbers in the Gospels themselves by the authors of the Greek New Testament. This book demonstrates unequivocally that the 'Sacred Union' of Jesus and his Lost Bride was the true cornerstone of early Christianity.

Like Brown she is keen to see the sacred feminine restored to the church, but her approach is certainly not mainstream. Brown also draws on Elaine Pagels, a major expert on the Gnostic gospels and on the original translation team. She believes that they represent a genuine early tradition in which Mary was prominent. Pagels, Starbird and Richard McBrien of Notre Dame University were all drawn on as scholars supporting Brown's use of the Gnostic gospels by ABC News in the US when it ran an investigation of the Code in November 2003. Similarly, ABC found scholarly support for Brown's interpretation of Da Vinci's last supper from Carlos Pedretti, one of the world's leading Leonardo experts and head of the Leonardo Institute in Florence. However, ABC noted, his voice was rare.

The implications of the ideas Brown draws together if true would, of course, lead to a rethinking of Christian tradition, and, as Brown has stated, this is clearly what he wants. In the end if the Code is offering us what Brown believes to be the true Jesus and the true Christian faith, Brown's Jesus is not a divine figure but a human who marries and has children. He is not a celibate Jew, but a believer in goddess worship and sacred sex. He is not someone who saves us by his blood but someone who failed in his plan to produce a new Davidic bloodline to sit on the throne of Israel.

If this is not the Jesus of traditional Christianity, it is, as Raj Persaud recognizes in the ITV 'Grail Trail,' a vision of Jesus that is far more appealing to many today. Equally 'code culture' means that those attracted to this Jesus and the sacred feminine are likely to find Brown's evidence convincing and dismiss Christian counterarguments as part of a conspiracy to hide the truth. At the end of the novel when Langdon kneels in worship to the Goddess, who we are told is returning to our world, we are clearly invited to do the same. How then should Christians respond?[31]

Running Events Based on The Da Vinci Code

4

With the film's release in May 2006, the debate started by the Code has a considerable new wind.

How can Christians run events that enter into the debate, enable their own beliefs to get a positive response, and not be seen as part of a conspiracy to silence the truth?

The Event You Should Not Run

The venue is a church hall; outside is a poster saying 'the wages of sin is death.' Most of the people attending are church members, most of whom have not read *The Da Vinci Code*. The non-Christians are few and are sympathetic to the book, which most of them have read and a number thoroughly enjoyed. There is only one speaker, the church minister. He has not read the book either but has read a number of books by Christians denouncing it. The evening consists of a talk by the minister in which he goes through a long list of facts that prove *The Da Vinci Code* is riddled with errors. He quotes book reviews that poor scorn on its bad writing style, some lead the church members to laughter and the minister joins in saying 'it's amazing anyone bothers to read this rubbish isn't it'? Then there is a time for questions. By now almost no-one will dare support any of the book's ideas. The minister responds to the few who do by quoting Scripture. He then concludes with a presentation of the cross and the true meaning of the blood of Jesus and makes an altar call. No-one responds. The Christians go home reassured that they can ignore *The Da Vinci Code*, the non-Christians go home convinced Brown must be onto something if the minister is so dismissive of the book.

Key Points in Running a Good Event

1 Be Prepared for a Genuine Debate

Brown's views touch on areas where Christians do not all agree. Indeed he and some of his sources view themselves as restoring the true Christian faith. This makes a genuine debate doubly scary because the Christians present may disagree on

It might be tempting to ensure that a party line is toed, but it is a temptation to avoid

important issues. It might be tempting to ensure that a party line is toed, but it is a temptation to avoid. Actually to hear that Christians do not all agree is likely to make Christianity more appealing to those the event will attract.

Remember that some of those present are likely to know of different Christian views, even just from reading the novel; any attempt to veto some opinions is likely to be exposed. Needless to say you, like me, are likely to consider some views as inconsistent with Christianity. If such views are raised treat them seriously but explain gently why for you they do not seem compatible with the Christian faith. It is also important that those attending are allowed to ask questions and that their views are taken seriously.

You also need to have read the book.

2 Try to Ensure There is Not Only One Speaker

Personally I would always like to have at least one speaker who was a supporter of much or all of Brown's ideas and able to argue his side of the argument. This will ensure better questions and will help you really engage with the issues and not come over as trying to do a cover up. Unfortunately finding people to do this may not be easy. You might, however, find someone to act as an interviewer for your Christian speaker or speakers and be able to push Brown's points in the way a news reporter will argue the opposite side to get a good interview. Better still get a local celebrity news person and use this to sell the event.

> *Better still get a local celebrity news person and use this to sell the event*

In an event run by Robin Gamble, Canon Evangelist at Manchester Cathedral, this was addressed by having a panel representing different issues, a Roman Catholic priest, a New Testament scholar, a leading female priest and an expert on the resurrection. These were interviewed in turn and then took audience questions. I would have suggested a non-Christian historian as another good panel member. If you go for a panel format it is certainly good to try and have a non-Christian, to have a Roman Catholic and a woman minister. Ideally one of the Christians should be sympathetic to a feminist agenda.

3 Chose Your Venue Wisely

The venue needs to be either atmospheric or neutral and welcoming. At Manchester they held it in the Cathedral, often used for public events but also having lots of atmosphere and its own share of cryptic looking art and artefacts. They had also considered the local Waterstones, which would have proved another good venue. For others it might be the local pub.[32] In New-castle they are exploring having a discussion after a showing of the film at an arts cinema—an excellent suggestion, which also allows the film to speak on Brown's behalf as a 'celluloid speaker.' The DVD will also enable discussion showings of the film, but remember you will need a licence to show it in public even at a free event!

4 Seek to Address the Following Key Issues in Your Event...
...in no particular order:

1 Would it have been wrong for Jesus to be married?

2 Has the church excluded women? What should be the place of women in the church?

3 Is sex evil?

4 Can we commune with God through sex or nature?

5 Is God male or best seen as a Goddess?

6 Are there descendents of Jesus alive today?

7 Do the Gnostic Gospels represent the true original Christian message?

8 Did the church deliberately suppress these books?

9 Did the church suppress Pagan beliefs?

10 How do you think we should view Mary Magdalene?

You and your speakers/panel members will need to decide how they respond to these issues. Below, in very rudimentary form, are some things I might say. You may not agree but I hope it helps your thinking.

1 Would it have been wrong for Jesus to be married?
Jesus was very much a human being and will have been attracted to women like any other man. Many of the apostles were married and it would not have been wrong for Jesus to marry either. However, the writings we have often depict Jesus predicting his death, so it might have been rather unkind to marry someone only to leave them a widow a couple of years later, particularly as widows had a very difficult time in Jesus' day.

2 Has the church excluded women? What should be the place of women in the church?
I think the church has excluded women in the past. In this it has gone along with the rest of society. Christians do not all agree on women's roles, but I think Jesus intended to have women in equal position to men. His female followers are the first he appears to at his resurrection and the ones who

stayed with him at his death. They travelled with Jesus and some of them funded his ministry. Paul says that in Christ there is no distinction between Jews and non-Jews, slaves and free people, and men and women—all are one in Christ. In his day he fought hard to get non-Jews accepted as equal. Two hundred years ago Christians were campaigning for freedom for slaves; now I believe it is important to see women equal to men in the church and I think Dan Brown is right to want this.

3 Is sex evil?
In the book Langdon suggests we need to look at sex as something sacred; for me this is actually a Christian response. Indeed, this is why Christians have often argued for sex only to be within marriage. It is something to be treated as special and only to be shared with those who are special to us. Sometimes Christians have treated sex as evil or as the way sin is passed on. To me this seems to have more to do with Greek ideas which saw bodies as evil, rather than the Christian and Jewish view that bodies are made by God and sex is God's gift.

4 Can we commune with God through sex or nature?
I think we can experience God in the world because I believe God is its source. God is, I think, also experienced our relationships with other people. Indeed, Christian mystics have often described relating to God in sexual terms. However, it seems to be getting the cart before the horse to suggest we ought to have sex in order to commune with God as the Code does. It seems to me sex is first and foremost about the relationship with the other person, so I would not support the kind of sex rites Brown talks about in the book.

5 Is God male or best seen as a Goddess?
Christians do not all agree on the language we should use for God but few would see God as male. The Bible begins by telling us God made humans male and female in God's image, so it makes sense to view God as being the source of both. God, however, is not a human, so in one sense talking of God having any gender is a human attempt to speak of God. However, I do sometimes think we have underused the female language for God in the Christian and Jewish tradition and this has led to a male biased view of God at times. I think we would gain a deeper understanding of God if we consciously related to the female as well as the male imagery. Contemporary Pagans view the balance between gods and goddesses as very important. As a Christian I believe there is only one divine being, so we cannot add a goddess to a god. Rather I think it is important that God is viewed as equally female and male.

6 Are there descendents of Jesus alive today?
I do not think Jesus had any children. There were Jewish groups at Jesus' time who did not marry so it was not as unusual as people think. However,

Christianity tells us that Jesus makes it possible for everyone to be children of God like him. So in a sense his blood is passed on to us. In fact that is the symbolism of drinking wine representing Jesus' blood at communion; his blood flows in our veins so we can be like Jesus. So I suppose on that basis I am a descendent of Jesus alive today, as could any of us be if we chose to follow him.

7 Do the Gnostic gospels represent the true original Christian message?

The people who wrote the Gnostic gospels certainly believed they were representing the truth and some scholars would view them as an original form of Christianity. Most would say, though, that the ideas in them seem to be later and not earlier than the traditional gospels; certainly the texts we have are later, though that does not prove there were not earlier texts we do not have. With regard to *The Da Vinci Code* the irony is that the Gnostic gospels, whilst they do give more prominence to female apostles, in other areas are more against Jesus' humanity and sex than the traditional ones. Many Gnostics believed that creation was made by an evil God and so nature was evil and that female sexuality was the tool used by evil to seduce human spirits into bondage in human bodies. These ideas turn up in various places in the Gnostic gospels. In line with this Jesus is viewed sometimes as not truly human either. In contrast I think the Bible teaches that creation is made by the same God who was in Jesus and that God plans to heal and transform creation through Jesus just as he offers this to people who seek it from him. That Jesus was both God and a real human being also shows us that bodies are good.

8 Did the church deliberately suppress these books?

The church did exclude Gnostic books from the Bible. However, most Christians at the time viewed Gnosticism as a new idea contrary to what Jesus taught rather than an original view they were replacing as some like Dan Brown suggest. Sadly, the church has in the past had a very poor record of brutality to those it viewed as heretics, and I suspect this has a lot to do with Christianity becoming a state religion, making it an act of treason to think differently about faith. I am glad we live in a world where free speech is allowed and think it important for Christians to allow people to air all sorts of views and respect those views. This does not mean we cannot disagree with them though.

9 Did the church suppress Pagan beliefs?

The church's approach to Pagan beliefs is varied. In some cases Christians have seen parallels in these beliefs, which is why many Pagan festivals were incorporated in Christianity. However, in other areas Christians did oppose them. Unfortunately there has been persecution of people for Pagan beliefs in Christian history. I think it is important today for Christians to respect

Pagans and support their acceptance as a serious religion, even if we do not agree with all they believe.

10 How do you think we should view Mary Magdalene?
Mary Magdalene is I think one of the key apostles of the Bible. Unfortunately in the West she has been hampered by being wrongly connected to the prostitute who anointed Jesus—a position that the Catholic church rejected in 1969, by the way. In the East she is viewed as the person who first preached Jesus to the Roman Emperor and she is the origin of their red Easter egg tradition. Mary used the egg to explain the idea of Jesus' resurrection to the Emperor who retorted that it was as likely for someone to rise from death as the egg to turn red. At this point the egg (reportedly) turned red. Mary is one of many female saints it would be really good to bring to prominence as a much needed role model. Her importance, however, rests on her being the key witness to Jesus' resurrection and her going out to spread the good news that by his death and resurrection Jesus had overcome death and evil, not on whether or not she was married to Jesus. Indeed it seems to me rather sexist to suggest the only way a women can become important is based on who she marries.

Appendix

Further Exploration

If you want to explore further I recommend two books. *Da Vinci Code Decoded* by Martin Lunn (The Disinformation Company, 2004). An expert historian reveals the truth behind Brown's research. It is non-dogmatic and not out to discredit Brown's *The Da Vinci Code* for religious motives. And Dan Burstein (ed), *Secrets of the Code* (CDS Books, 2004) is unusual in being a collection of experts sympathetic to the book (and several are Brown's sources). These will help you get into the issues and cannot be accused of being part of a church conspiracy, as can the numerous books written by Christians, many of which are also well researched. Opus Dei have issued a measured response at www.opusdei.org. It will not answer all their critics but does point out some glaring errors in Brown's book, notably that there are no monks in Opus Dei. There is also a lot of information at

- http://www.channel4.com/culture/microsites/W/weirdworlds/da_vinci_code/index.html
- http://en.wikipedia.org/wiki/The_Da_Vinci_Code

A site more sympathetic to Brown is

- http://altreligion.about.com/library/bl_davincicode.htm

Some Key Facts[33]

- Some Gnostic gospels do make Mary Magdalene important, but do not say Jesus and Mary were married or that they kissed on the mouth, though a section of manuscript is missing at this point.
- The Gnostic gospels are usually considered to be later than the four in the Bible, though a few serious scholars doubt this.
- The Dead Sea Scrolls are pre-Christian texts and say nothing about Jesus or Mary as Brown claims.

- It is claimed as a Rabbi Jesus must have married. However, rabbinical Judaism is later than Jesus' day when there were many different forms. Groups like the Essenes, who share a number of things in common with Jesus, were celibate, so it would not have been unthinkable for Jesus to be single.

- Pope Gregory did mistakenly combine several biblical women to make Mary a prostitute in 591. The Catholic Church has since rejected this at the second Vatican council of 1969. Some iconography and writing also shows that the western church made her at times symbolic of female sexual sin. The East has always rejected this tradition and Protestants have rarely accepted it.

- Leonardo Da Vinci never wrote anything about Jesus' marriage or the Holy Grail. Brown's ideas are modern theories with no record in Leonardo's day. Leonardo was indeed unorthodox and homosexual but almost certainly did not paint Grail codes into his paintings.

- The original Grail in the legends was not the chalice of the last supper; it was the name given to a bowl in which Joseph of Arimathea was supposed to have gathered Jesus' blood at the cross.

- The word for Holy Grail in French *sangraal* cannot be rendered *san grael* and thus cannot mean *sang rael*, holy blood. The mistake comes from an English copy of the legend which got the French wrong.

- The Priory of Sion was a real organization, registered by Piere Plantard who claimed to be the Merovingian royal descendent. However, it has no reliable history prior to 1956. The documents in the Paris library were admitted to be forgeries by Plantard during a trial in 1993. He made them to create a false genealogy.

- 5 million women were not burnt as witches by the church. It is hardly edifying to record witch trial deaths at 50,000 at most, but true. And many of these were not women and the majority were not burned by the church but by small rural communities in Protestant Germany. The Catholic Church did set up the Inquisition to root out heresy and targeted women, Protestants, Muslims and Jews unpleasantly and inexcusably, but this is not Brown's claim.

- The Knights Templar did become very powerful and were destroyed by Philip IV on a charge of devil worship. However, it is highly unlikely they dug 50 metres under the Temple to recover documents from Jesus' time (or even further to uncover magic books of King Solomon as others have suggested). There is no evidence for such a massive dig. They did not build churches either.

Notes

1 'The Grail trail; in pursuit of the Da Vinci Code.'

2 'Dismantling The Da Vinci Code,' *Crisis Magazine*, 2003 (Morley Publishing Group, Inc).

3 See David Hay and Kate Hunt, *The Spirituality of People Who Don't Go To Church* (Nottingham University, 2000).

4 See S Hollinghurst, *New Age, Paganism and Christian Mission* (Grove Evangelism booklet, Ev 64).

5 To explore this area further you may wish to look at P Beckley, *Mission in a Conspiracy Culture* (Grove Evangelism booklet, Ev 60).

6 Milan, 1989, current English edition Vintage, 2001.

7 www.danbrown.com

8 It is often forgotten because *The Da Vinci Code* is the first of Brown's novels to be a big success that he has written three previous novels. All have elements of conspiracy theory and the cracking of codes and also contain discussions of religion. *The Da Vinci Code* is in fact the second book centred on the character of Robert Langdon, following on from *Angels and Demons,* and is part of an intended series with him as central character.

9 See pp 42–43.

10 See pp 60–63.

11 See pp 72–74.

12 See pp 128–135.

13 PHI is the name for the 'Divine Proportion,' a number claimed to govern natural ratios.

14 p 134.

15 See p 158.

16 p 172.

17 p 173.

18 How this also leads to Orthodox Jews and Islam rejecting women, as the passage also claims, Brown does not explain.

19 pp 409–413.

20 p 413.

21 For more on Wicca, Paganism and New Age and how they relate to each other see S Hollinghurst, *New Age, Paganism and Christian Mission* (Grove Evangelism booklet, Ev64).

22 See p 355.

23 pp 67–8.

24 See for instance Sister Sandrine's comment on p 178.

25 Bearing in mind Brown is an American I wonder if his target here is actually US conservative Christianity and the debate of evolution teaching in schools.

26 pp 206–7.

27 Michael Baigent, Richard Leigh and Henry Lincoln (Arrow, 2004) originally published 1982.

28 The major discussion of this comes on pp 312–350 where Langdon and Teabing explain the true Grail to Sophie.

29 www.telisphere.com/~starbird/

30 See his website www.danbrown.com

31 See pages 581 and 592.

32 See P Howell-Jones, N Wills, *Pints of View: Encounters Down the Pub* (Grove Evangelism booklet, Ev72) for ideas on running such events.

33 I have ignored a whole raft of geographical or descriptive inaccuracies that some cite. Whilst some of these belie Browns' claim to have accurately described architecture and artwork, most would attract little attention in any other novel and are not really crucial to his thesis.